The Backwoods Chronicles: Freddy Fox's Freaky Fire

A Story About the Importance of Mentorship

by
Lawrence Carey, Robert A. Carey, Psy.D.
and Debra Warner, Psy.D.

Published by Dr. Debra Publishing

Copyright 2022 Lawrence Carey, Robert A. Carey, Psy.D. & Debra Warner, Psy.D.

All Rights Reserved.

No part of this book may be reproduced in any form whatsoever, by photography or xerography or by any other means, by broadcast or transmission electronically or otherwise without permission in writing from the publisher or authors, except by a reviewer who may quote brief passages in critical articles or reviews.

Dr. Debra Publishing
979-8-218-02948-7

Printed in the United States
1st Printing 2022

ATTENTION: ORGANIZATIONS & CORPORATIONS
Bulk quantity discounts for reselling, gifts or fundraising are available. For more information, please contact SCRIPT@consultant.com

Cover Design and Illustrations: Dave Warner

Dedication
To Aunt Susie

Acknowledgments

We acknowledge all who supported us in this process and wanted more Backwoods Chronicles! Look for our next chronicle in 2023.

From Lawrence Carey

This book represents that people can achieve anything. It also shows that sometimes you need others to show you the way.

**From Robert Carey, Psy.D.
and Debra Warner, Psy.D.**

This book represents our relationship within our family and how we all work together to get things done. We can accomplish anything! How blessed are we. Thank you again, heavenly Father, for blessing us.

Table of Contents

Preface	1
The Story	2
Summary	14
Epilogue	15
About the Authors	16

Preface

The Importance of This Book

According to Lawrence
This book is the second in a series of stories regarding work management and types of people. It's about how people behave and interact in a social context in the workplace. In this book, you will learn about applying organizational psychology principles. It continues the animal classifications from the first book *Beavers, Foxes, Grizzly Bears...Oh, and Cheetahs, Fish and Sloths Too*. It is important so that people understand how they need others and how teamwork and diversity help complete tasks.

According to Debra Warner, Psy.D.
This book continues an idea I had over 17 years ago. I never thought I would be writing a book series with my son. This book is important because it teaches more than the subject matter. It shows how to mentor your children for success.

The Story

Freddy Fox's Freaky Fire

Freddie Fox fidgeted feverishly before fumbling the phone as he finished his call. "Finally!" he exclaimed. "Everyone will know what a master of management Freddie Fox really is."

Most of the team was already gathered in the conference room for the weekly staff meeting when Freddie sauntered on to the scene.

"Bad news, builders. Billy Beaver got bacteria from a bundle of bad birch wood. It looks like he'll be laying low for a little while. Benny and the bears are hibernating and as you already know, Sonya Sloth is sightseeing with her sister in Schenectady, so we'll be a little shorthanded for a few days. On top of all that, I just heard that Mr. Lawrence T. Lion is bringing some big muckety-muck investor here this afternoon to show off our latest project, the Backwoods branch of Big Bob's Burrito Bakery."

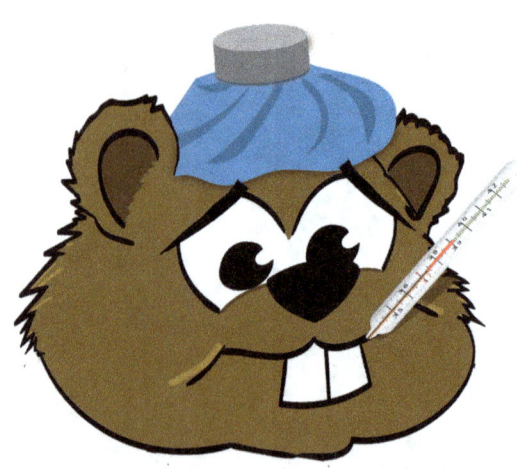

The team turned toward each other in trepidation as an air of apprehension enveloped the room. The Fabulous Five were frightened, except for Phil who hadn't made it to the meeting yet, but Clive Cougar was the first to call out concern.

"Um, Freddie, how are we supposed to prepare for a visit from the VIPs without Billy and Sonya to help keep us on track?"

"No need to worry or Freddie Fox isn't furry. I, the maestro of management, the legend of leadership, the captain of competence will keep things running like a well-oiled machine."

"But Freddie," countered Clive, "you never attended any of the management trainings and you didn't even participate in the mentorship program. I seem to remember you saying, 'What in the woods do I need that junk for?'"

"Yeah," chimed in Chelsea Cheetah, "then you said, those who can, do. Those who can't, get a mentor."

"Fret not, my feline friends. Never fear, my fishy fellows. Our lion leadership literally left me large and in charge. Clearly, cool cats can corroborate my qualifications to captain this crew. Can you?"

"Oh Lawrrrd," lamented Freeda Fish. "The lions only let you lord over the lake shore because Billy Beaver got botulism while Benny and the bears are bedded down in their dens during their seasonal slumber..."

BOOM!

A deafening disturbance disrupted Freeda's dialog. The walls wobbled, the windows wiggled, and the ceiling fan swung side to side. Frantically, fox, fish, and felines alike fled to the freedom of the forest outside.

"F-f-f-FIRE!," fretted Freddy.

The Backwoods branch of Big Bob's Burrito Bakery was a brightly burning bundle of boards.

Phil Fish floated feebly ashore. His fishbowl fractured, he was gasping at the gills.

"Quickly," cried Caitlin, "he can't breathe without water!"

"Somebody, do something!" shouted Freddy.

"I know!" chimed in Chuck Cheetah, "there's a firehose at the fifty-foot fir tree."

"That won't work," whimpered Chandler Cheetah.

"Why not?" wondered Chuck.

"We can't work the water faucets. None of us have opposable thumbs."

Finally, Fernando Fish found his voice. "Um, guys, you know we can just roll him back into the water, right?"

"Perfect!" proclaimed Freddy. "But the bakery is still burning."

Suddenly the sly fox's cellphone signaled someone was calling.

"How's y'all doing?" said Sonya Sloth in a southern accent.

"How are we doing?" Freddy was flabbergasted.

He stammered several syllables, but the only words Sonya could make out were "bakery" and "burning."

"Did you call Gary Gorilla's fire and cleanup crew?" Sonya asked. "His number is on Billy Beaver's desk. You would know that Freddy, if you had let Billy mentor you like he wanted to. Just call Gary. It will cost you a bunch of bananas, but Gary's gang will have everything shipshape by sundown."

Soon strange sounds started seeping from the forest. Noises not known before in the Backwoods bellowed boisterously while shadowy figures flittered and fluttered in the fir trees.

"Come now! What kind of creatures can they be?" cried Caitlin.

Freddie crinkled his keen canine eyes. "Can't say for sure but they've got lots of gear."

"Gear?" queried Clive.

"Gizmos, gadgets, all types of tools."

"Tools, you say? They have tools? That means they must have ... THUMBS! It must be that Gary guy and his gang of gorillas. Goodness gracious, what glorious news. Oh, thumbs! I can't wait to see them in action. I've always wanted thumbs myself of course, but this is almost as auspicious. Just think of the things that can be done with thumbs."

"Yeah, if you had thumbs, you could hitch a ride out of here," chided Chelsea.

Rapidly, the riotous ruckus rolled up in front of the team.

"Greetings," grinned a gargantuan gorilla. "I'm Gary. We heard you had some combustion in your construction. It looks like your timber turned to tinder. But don't bother about it, we'll battle that blaze for bananas. I brought the whole crew, so we'll need more than a few."

"Sure," said Freddie. "We'll get right on that."

"Primates, prepare to pounce," Gary grunted to his gang.

And the troop trotted triumphantly toward the billowing blaze.

"I hope they're fast," Chandler fretted to Freddie. "Lawrence Lion should be landing in exactly eight hours."

Seven hours and fifty-nine minutes later, Gary and his gang grabbed their bananas, grunted their goodbyes, and the hairy hooligans hurried happily home.

Just then a helicopter hovered over the horizon. Lawrence Lion landed on the lawn along with the rest of the board and the highfalutin' financier. Freddie Fox feared the worst, but he presented the project with poise and professionalism.

When the tour terminated, Mr. Lion talked to the team. "The Backwoods branch of Big Bob's Burrito Bakery is beyond beautiful," he boasted. "I'm sure Billy Beaver is beaming with pride at the work you have done here. Say, where is Mr. Beaver today?"

"Sadly, sir, he is suddenly sick. Spoiled sap I suppose, from a bad batch of birchwood," Freddie explained.

"Well, please extend my best wishes for a speedy recovery. It's a credit to his leadership skills that you all can continue your fine work even in his absence. This team runs like a well-oiled machine."

With that he waved goodbye and flew off into the sunset.

Freddie Fox's phone rang. It was Sonya Sloth.

"How'd it go?" she asked.

"Well, all's well that ends well, right? But I promise that I'll sign up for those management trainings tomorrow, and when Billy Beaver gets better, I will ask him to please be my mentor."

As the sun set, Freddie sat by the shore savoring some solitude when Franky and Felix Fish floated leisurely along.

"How's Phil?" Freddie asked.

"Phil's fine," Franky replied. "He just needs to rest for a day or two."

"Was he able to say what happened?"

"He said some guy from the human construction company downstream gave him something called 'dynamite.' It's supposed to dig holes faster. But Phil couldn't hold onto the thing called a detonator and when he dropped it, everything went BOOM."

"Couldn't hold on to it? Why not?"

"Phil said, it was because he doesn't have thumbs."

The End

Summary

All animals can be parts of others. People in organizations often are, but people are easier to manage when they are one or the other. However, we are made up of differences. This book expresses the importance of allowing your employees to be who they are in your organization. It illustrates how problematic it can be for employees who are not properly trained. Moreover, while we can train, mentorship is also key for an employees' effectiveness.

Epilogue

As he clicks the sign-up button, Freddy says frustratedly under his breath, "Never, never again".

About the Authors

Lawrence Carey
Lawrence is a sixth-grade student who enjoys math and science. His dream is to become a paleontologist. However, for right now he settles for being a human marvel encyclopedia and playing with his faithful dog Orion, "the force puppy."

Robert A. Carey, Psy.D. (Daddy)
Dr. Robert A. Carey is a clinical forensic psychologist and conservatorship supervisor. He has worked with a variety of client populations, including foster children, adult survivors of abuse and people with severe mental illness. As a survivor himself, he devotes his career to assisting diverse populations of trauma. In his spare time, he focuses on his family, which includes building "ginormous" castles, play coffins and "sparklies" for his wife Dr. Debra.

Debra Warner, Psy.D. (Ma Ma)
Dr. Debra Warner is a Professor the Listen & Love University. Her areas of expertise include: male survivors related to trauma and violence, community gang intervention, immigration and mental health, competency, psychological testing, diversity, personality disorders, and substance abuse. Dr. Warner is a frequent speaker at conferences and other venues. Check out her TedX Talk called *Breaking the Silence of Male Trauma Survivors*. She is involved in social media and is an often-quoted expert in books, television and radio.